Where Is
California?

Where Is California?

by Jennifer Marino Walters

illustrated by Ted Hammond

Penguin Workshop

To Keith, Matt, Nate, and Lily: Thank you for all
your support and for being my biggest fans!—JMW

PENGUIN WORKSHOP
An imprint of Penguin Random House LLC
1745 Broadway, New York, NY 10019
penguinrandomhouse.com

Designed and Produced by Dinardo Design, LLC.

Library of Congress Cataloging-in-Publication Data is available.

First published in the United States of America by Penguin Workshop, 2025

Manufactured in the United States of America
CJKW

ISBN 9798217051281 (paperback)
10 9 8 7 6 5 4 3 2 1

ISBN 9798217051298 (library binding)
10 9 8 7 6 5 4 3 2 1

The authorized representative in the EU for product safety and compliance is
Penguin Random House Ireland, Morrison Chambers, 32 Nassau Street,
Dublin D02 YH68, Ireland, https://eu-contact.penguin.ie.

Contents

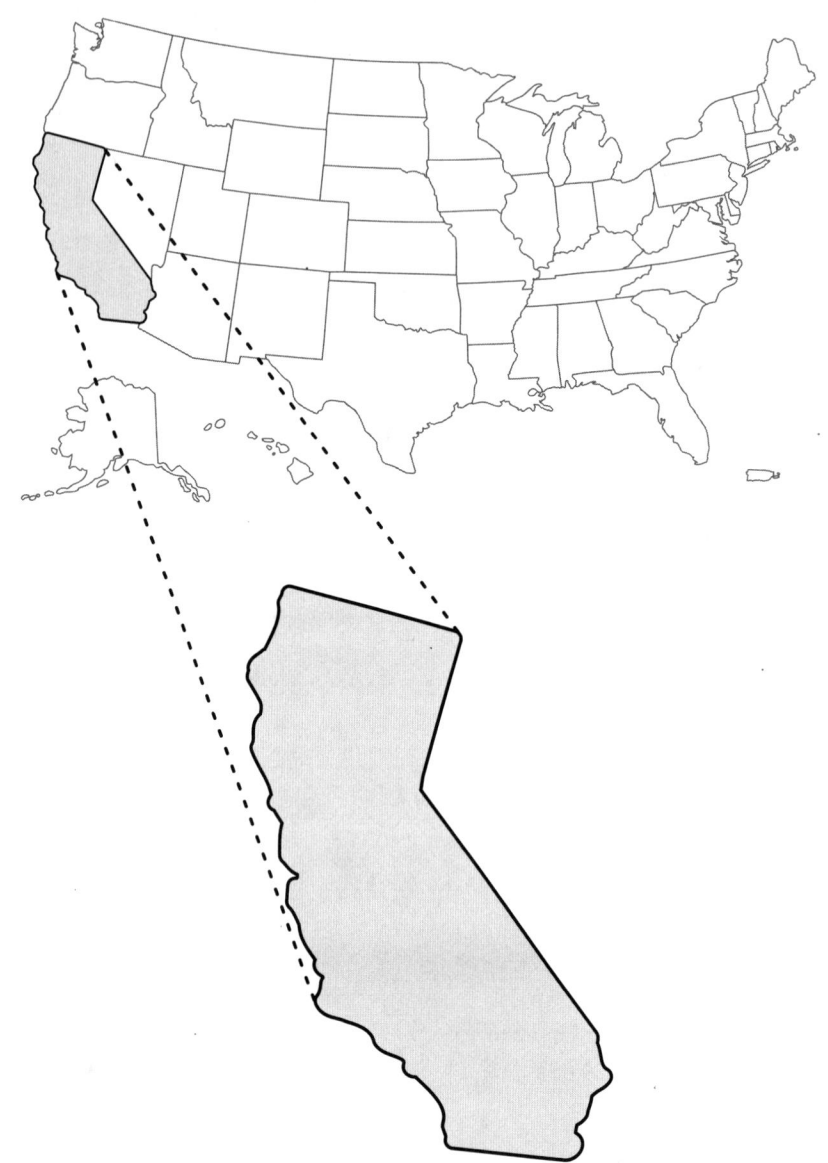

Where Is California?

California is a land of extremes. The lowest point in the United States, the highest point on the US mainland, and the hottest place on earth are all found in California. California has the biggest population, the largest economy, and the most biological diversity of any US state. Some of the world's tallest trees, highest waterfalls, deepest valleys, and active volcanoes are found there.

A typical day in California can be full of extremes. Can you imagine skiing on a snowy mountain and then lounging on a sunny beach all in one day? You can do it in California!

CHAPTER 1
California's Land and Environment

California is a huge state—the third largest in the United States, after Alaska and Texas. At 163,695 square miles, it's bigger than many countries, including Japan and Italy. And within the state there is a wide range of terrains, climates, and ecosystems.

California is located on the West Coast of the United States. It is bordered by the Pacific Ocean to the west, Nevada and Arizona to the east, Oregon to the north, and the country of Mexico to the south.

There are four natural regions of California. The first, the coastal region, includes hundreds of miles of amazing coastline along the Pacific Ocean. Southern California is known for its wide, sandy beaches. In Central California, the coastline contains rocky cliffs that drop straight into the ocean. The temperature in the southern coastal region is typically warm, with dry summers and occasionally wet winters. Temperatures are cooler farther north along the coast, especially in winter. In San Francisco, for example, the temperature can dip below 50 degrees Fahrenheit.

California's second and middle region, the Central Valley, is the center of the state's agricultural production. That's because the most fertile land in the state is found there. Over one-third of the vegetables, and nearly 75 percent of the fruits and nuts in the United States, are grown in California. That's over four hundred crops in total! Some of the state's largest harvests are grapes, almonds, lettuce, and strawberries.

The Central Valley is very hot and dry in the summer and foggy in the winter. The state's two longest rivers, the San Joaquin River and the

Sacramento River, run through it.

The third region of California is made up of its mountain ranges. The coastal ranges, including the Klamath Mountains in the state's northwest corner, separate the coastal region from the Central Valley. The inland mountain ranges include the Cascades in north-central and northeast California and the Sierra Nevada in the

eastern-central part of the state. The mountain areas have short summers and cold winters.

Finally, there's the fourth region—the desert region, which takes up most of eastern California. The Mojave Desert, located in the southeastern part of the state, is home to Death Valley, the hottest place on earth and the driest place in North America. Death Valley also contains the

lowest point in the United States, Badwater Basin, which sits 282 feet below sea level. (Interestingly, California is also home to the highest point on the US mainland, Mount Whitney, in the Sierra Nevada. It towers about 14,500 feet above sea level.)

Two other major California deserts, both in the southeast, are the Colorado Desert and the Great Basin Desert. Like all deserts, California's deserts are very dry.

With such a wide range of geography, it's no surprise that California is home to a huge variety of plants and animals. It is more biologically diverse than any other US state, with about forty thousand plant and animal species.

About one-third of California is covered in forests, containing mostly conifers (trees that produce cones) like pine trees, cedar trees, and California's famous giant redwoods and sequoias. You'll also find palm trees along the coast and in other areas, although most of them have been imported from outside the state.

Some of California's most plentiful land animals are brown bears, wildcats, cougars, deer, coyotes, black bears, skunks, and raccoons. The Pacific Ocean off California's coast is home to a huge variety of marine life, including tuna, bass, rockfish, sharks, and rays. Marine mammals such as dolphins, seals, sea otters, whales, and sea lions also live there. Millions of people flock to San Diego's La Jolla Cove in Southern California and San Francisco's Pier 39 in Northern California to see its resident sea lions basking in the sun. Whale watching cruises are also popular.

Unfortunately, many animal species in California are endangered. These include the famed California condor, the largest land bird in North America. Other animals, like the California grizzly bear, are now extinct. In fact, California is the only US state with an image of an extinct

animal—the California grizzly—on its state flag and seal.

In addition to its various landforms, California is home to thousands of lakes. Lake Tahoe, which sits on the California-Nevada border in the Sierra

Nevada, is the second-deepest lake in the United States. The Salton Sea in Southern California (a saltwater lake) is the largest lake in the state. Clear Lake, north of San Francisco, is its biggest freshwater lake.

California's National Parks

National parks are large areas of land set aside by the government to protect natural and historic resources. There are sixty-three national parks in the United States, and California has nine of them—more than any other state. They contain some amazing geological treasures. Here are a few:

Death Valley National Park is the largest US national park outside of Alaska, covering 3.4 million acres. There you'll find giant sand dunes, deep canyons, and huge salt flats (flat areas of land covered with salt and other minerals).

Yosemite National Park is in the heart of the Sierra Nevada. It's known for its spectacular waterfalls, including Yosemite Falls, which plummets 2,425 feet. It's also home to the famous Half Dome, a massive granite rock formation that's over 8,800 feet above sea level. Also in the Sierra

Nevada is Sequoia National Park. Its giant sequoia trees are some of the largest living things on earth.

Redwood National Park, located on California's northern coast, is famous for its towering redwood trees. Its lush forests contain 45 percent of the world's old-growth redwoods. That includes the tallest living redwood tree, Hyperion, standing about 380 feet tall. That's taller than the Statue of Liberty!

California is located on the Ring of Fire, a horseshoe-shaped belt around the Pacific Ocean that's home to three-quarters of the world's active volcanoes. Several of them are in California. These include the 14,163-foot Mount Shasta and the 10,456-foot Lassen Peak, both part of Northern California's Cascade Range. About 90 percent of earthquakes in the world occur around the Ring of Fire.

California is also prone to wildfires, due in large part to the warm, dry climate in much of the state. Santa Ana winds—strong, extremely dry winds that start in the area east of the Sierra Nevada and blow west toward the Pacific Ocean—can spark wildfires and help them spread faster, destroying trees and brush. Then, rain or melting snow can cause water to rush down mountains and create mudslides and flash floods.

In California, there is potential for earthquakes, wildfires, and other extreme weather events. Still, people have chosen to live there for thousands of years. Its first settlers came from Asia in search of warmer weather. Eventually, there were hundreds of Indigenous nations, including the Mojave and Washoe, living in what is now California. Today, many Indigenous people and nations make their homes there.

But California didn't officially become a US state until September 9, 1850, when it became the country's thirty-first state. And over centuries, it has grown to be the most populous state, home to over thirty-nine million people as of 2024.

CHAPTER 2
State Origins

Most historians agree that California got its name from a 1500s Spanish novel about a fictional island paradise called California. And in fact, the Spanish were the first Europeans to arrive there.

In the early 1500s, Mexico was controlled by Spain. In 1542, a Spanish explorer named Juan Rodríguez Cabrillo sailed from the west coast of Mexico to San Diego Bay and claimed it for Spain.

English explorer Sir Francis Drake sailed across the Atlantic Ocean from England, around the southern tip of South America, and on to Northern California in 1579. He named that land New Albion and claimed it for England.

Another Spanish explorer, Sebastián Vizcaíno,

traveled along California's coast in 1602. He gave many places their current names—including San Diego in the south, Santa Barbara in central California, and Monterey in the north.

But California was mostly neglected by the Spanish until 1769. Fearful that European powers like Russia and England would seize the land, Spain sent a military expedition led by Gaspar de Portolá to build military forts (called presidios) along the coast. The group was also ordered to build missions (religious settlements) to convert members of Indigenous nations to Christianity and to teach them to speak Spanish and to farm and ranch.

Portolá built the first presidio in San Diego, and a Roman Catholic priest named Father Junípero Serra began the first mission (called Mission San Diego de Alcalá) there. This was officially the first Spanish settlement in California. By 1823, there were twenty-one missions and four presidios along California's coast. The Europeans were reinforcing their "ownership" of the land.

Many Indigenous people were enslaved and forced to live at these missions. Life in the missions was brutal for them. They worked long and hard on tasks like farming, building, and cooking for little or no reward. They received little education. If they broke rules, they endured severe punishments.

The Indigenous nations did not want to lose their languages, religions, and cultures. Some tried to escape. Others attempted to fight back. Many were beaten or killed. And thousands died from diseases the Spanish brought, like smallpox, chicken pox, and measles.

This was devastating to Indigenous nations. Before the Spanish arrived in California, close to three hundred thousand people were living there. By 1840, only about half of that number remained.

In 1821, the country of Mexico won its independence from Spain after fighting the Mexican Revolution. California was now part of Mexico. In 1833, the Mexican government began shutting down California's missions and dividing the lands around them (called ranchos) among the Spanish settlers. Some Indigenous people went to work for the new landowners. Others tried to return to their homelands, but in many cases, they were forced to relocate by white settlers.

The US government also wanted control of California. From the 1820s through the 1840s, Mexico and the United States argued over the land of California. Mexico refused to sell it.

In 1841, the first organized white American settlers arrived in California. They traveled from Missouri in search of rich farmland and a warm climate. Like the Spanish had done, the Americans forced more Indigenous nations off their land.

In June 1846, a group of Americans rebelled against Mexican rule in California. They raised a Bear Flag at a Mexican settlement in Sonoma, located in Northern California, and declared California an independent republic. The Bear Flag later became the official state flag in 1911.

But this independent California Republic lasted less than a month. In 1846, the United States and Mexico went to war. The United States won the Mexican-American War two years later, taking control of California and several other western states.

That's when California's population of settlers from the rest of the United States began to expand. On January 24, 1848, a man named James Marshall was building a sawmill (a place where logs are cut to make boards) in the foothills of the Sierra Nevada when he discovered something shiny: gold. Rumors of his discovery began to spread.

On December 5, 1848, President James K. Polk confirmed that the rumors were true. Like many Americans, he believed in Manifest Destiny—the idea that US citizens had the right and duty to spread out across the entire country from the East Coast to the West Coast.

In 1849, thousands of people trekked to California with the hope of striking it rich. These people were called forty-niners because of the year they set out. Their journey out west became known as the Gold Rush.

Most of the forty-niners settled in the

northern part of California, where the gold was originally found. They set up mining camps and worked long and hard under extremely difficult conditions. While a few of them found gold and become wealthy, most found nothing. The Gold Rush sparked a period of huge growth for California. By 1850, its population had grown from about 15,000 to nearly 100,000. By 1860, it ballooned to about 380,000. Many farms and ranches sprang up round the state.

The Gold Rush impacted the entire country, not just California. Chinese workers who had come to California in search of gold helped build the Transcontinental Railroad. Irish laborers also came to work on the railroad. Completed in 1869, the Transcontinental Railroad extended from the northeastern United States all the way to California. That meant people could travel from coast to coast in just one week.

One group the Gold Rush did not help were

the members of Indigenous nations. There were about 150,000 Indigenous people in California when the Gold Rush began. But by 1860, only 30,000 remained. For many, there was no choice but to try to blend in to the settlers' culture to survive.

CHAPTER 3
Growth and Development

Even after the Gold Rush ended, California continued to grow. This growth was due, in part, to the completion of the Transcontinental Railroad.

In 1883, a man named Harvey Henderson Wilcox and his wife, Daeida (known as Ida), traveled by train to Los Angeles in order to escape the cold winters in Kansas. Once settled, Harvey and Ida bought a large area of land just west of Los Angeles. They divided it into smaller parcels and sold them to wealthy people from the Midwest who wanted to build second homes in a warmer climate. Ida called the community "Hollywood," and soon everyone began referring to it that way.

By 1900, Los Angeles was a sizable, bustling

city with over one hundred thousand residents. Hollywood grew steadily, too, and in 1910 it became part of Los Angeles.

Many early filmmakers were attracted to Los Angeles and the surrounding area. The weather was ideal for filming outdoors all year long, and the scenery was varied, with beaches, mountains, deserts, and canyons. By the early 1920s,

Hollywood had become the film capital of the world and many big movie studios opened there.

Irish, French, and Italian immigrants had begun flocking to San Francisco during the Gold Rush and continued to settle there. Thousands of Mexican and Filipino people also came to California to find work on farms, where they spent long, hot hours in the sun for very little pay. The population of the state had already passed one million.

Another development in the early 1900s spurred population growth in California: the increased popularity of the automobile. As automobiles grew more common in the United States, the first transcontinental highway, called the Lincoln Highway, was mapped out in 1913. The highway made it possible for many more people to move across the country to California. Still more arrived after the completion of Route 66, a highway that ran from Chicago,

Illinois, to Los Angeles.

Then the Great Depression hit. Lasting about ten years, the Great Depression was an economic crisis that left many people in the United States without jobs and with very little money. Many families became homeless.

In the middle of the Great Depression, a drought (a long period of time during which there is little or no rain) descended on the Great Plains, an area in the center of the United States with many large farms. During the drought, high winds and dry soil created dust storms that ruined farmland and destroyed crops. The area became known as the Dust Bowl. Thousands of farming families from the region headed west to California, hoping to find better lives there. But many found low wages and poor conditions instead.

By the 1930s, many migrant farm workers in California began to organize strikes and boycotts

Cesar Chavez speaks to farm workers

to fight for higher wages and safer working conditions. In 1962, a Mexican American former farm worker named Cesar Chavez, along with Dolores Huerta and other organizers, formed a union called the United Farm Workers Association. The union organized peaceful protests and strikes to call attention to the problems migrant workers faced. Cesar Chavez's birthday, March 31, is now celebrated as a state holiday each year in California.

During World War II (1939–1945), California became a center for defense manufacturing, producing aircrafts, ships, and weapons. Military bases also sprang up throughout the state, including huge naval bases in San Diego. After the war, many workers in the military and defense industries remained in California, which led to more growth in large cities like Los Angeles, San Francisco, and San Diego. As families began to move to the suburbs around these cities, shopping malls, movie theaters, and supermarkets appeared.

This steady population growth brought about many of the changes that helped shape California into the state it is today. Huge multilane freeways were built to accommodate automobile traffic. Bridges were built, including the iconic

Golden Gate Bridge in San Francisco in 1937. Painted reddish orange—not gold—the bridge gets its name from the Golden Gate Strait, which it spans. Almost a mile long, the Golden Gate Bridge remains a symbol of California and one of the most popular US landmarks.

In the 1970s, California's technology industry exploded. Steve Wozniak and Steve Jobs created the first Apple computers in a garage in Los

Altos, near San Francisco, in 1976. Today, California is a world leader in producing computers, video games, and other electronics. The state's technology industry is centered in the San Francisco Bay Area's Silicon Valley, between Palo Alto and San Jose. Many major technology companies like Apple, Google, Hewlett Packard, and Intel are based there.

Today, over 75 percent of California residents

live in or near its three biggest cities, Los Angeles, San Francisco, and San Diego. But none of those is California's state capital. That honor belongs to Sacramento, a city of over 525,000 people in Northern California.

Sacramento officially became California's state capital in 1854. Prior to 1854, the capital had been San Jose (1849–51), Vallejo (1852–53), Sacramento briefly (1852), and Benicia (1853–54). A few different buildings served as the state capitol, the physical place where the government meets to conduct business, before it moved to its current building in Sacramento in 1869.

Like the US federal government, California has three branches of government. The executive branch is led by the governor. California has had two former Hollywood actors as governor. Ronald Reagan served from 1967 to 1975, before he became president of the United States in 1981, and Arnold Schwarzenegger served as governor from 2003 to 2011.

California's legislative branch consists of the eighty-person assembly and the forty-member state senate. The legislature meets in the capitol building, which also houses the governor's office. The third branch is the Supreme Court of California, which includes seven justices.

California's first constitution was drafted in 1849. A new constitution was adopted in 1879 and has since been amended (changed) over five hundred times. One unique change, added in 1911, allows California citizens to recall (remove) public officials they aren't happy with. This recall was used to remove Governor Gray Davis from office in 2003.

Because of its large population, California is also well represented in the United States House of Representatives. It has fifty-two US representatives, more than any other state.

California Quakes

Each year, California experiences thousands of earthquakes—about ten thousand in Southern California alone! Luckily, most of them are too small to be felt.

The earth's crust (outer layer) is made up of many tectonic plates—large slabs of rock that are constantly moving. An earthquake is formed when two tectonic plates scrape or bump against each other.

California experiences a large number of earthquakes. It's located on the boundaries of two tectonic plates, the Pacific Plate and the North American Plate. The main boundary of those plates is the San Andreas Fault, which runs south along the Northern California coast and moves inland in Southern California. There are thousands of recognized faults in California, but only a small

number pose a significant danger.

Though most earthquakes in California are small, there have been some major ones. One of the biggest was the San Francisco earthquake of 1906, which left at least half the city's people homeless and is estimated to have killed between eight hundred and three thousand people. Also significant was the San Francisco earthquake of 1989, which caused sixty-three deaths and injured more than three thousand people.

CHAPTER 4
California Today

California's population today is extremely diverse. About 40 percent of Californians are Latino, 35 percent are white, 15 percent are Asian American or Pacific Islander, 5 percent are Black, 4 percent are multiracial, and less than 1 percent are Native American or Alaska Natives. (Even though they are a small percentage, California is still home to more Native Americans than any other state.)

Over two hundred languages are spoken in California. English is the most common, followed by Spanish and Chinese (both Mandarin and Cantonese).

To accommodate California's large population, it has built up an extensive transportation system.

Even with their expansive freeway systems, major cities like Los Angeles still have heavy traffic. But there is also a subway system in Los Angeles, trolley systems in San Diego and San Francisco, and a train system connecting communities in the San Francisco Bay Area.

California has over thirty public universities. Ten of them are part of the University of California system, including UC Los Angeles (UCLA) and UC Berkeley. California also has over one hundred private universities. These include top schools like Stanford University in Palo Alto and the University of Southern California in Los Angeles.

California has the largest economy of any US state—larger than that of many countries! A city, state, or country's economy is the system through which goods and services are produced, bought, and sold.

California's booming economy has been shaped over many years. The aerospace, defense,

automobile, and technology industries still play a major role in California's economy, and Hollywood remains the center of American film and TV industries. It is watched over by the famous Hollywood sign in the nearby Hollywood Hills.

One of the biggest drivers of California's

economy is its tourism industry. Hundreds of millions of tourists flock to California each year. They hike in the scenic national parks, visit iconic cities like Los Angeles and San Francisco, and visit popular theme parks like Disneyland in Anaheim and Universal Studios Hollywood.

The Port of Los Angeles and the Port of Long

Beach are two of the country's busiest shipping ports for international trade.

California is also a music industry hub, and many major music labels are based there. The first big record label to establish itself in California was Capitol Records in 1942, now housed in the famous Capitol Records Tower in Hollywood. California has had an influence on many musical styles, from rock and roll to rhythm and blues. Its first signature sound, surf rock, was made popular in the 1960s by the band the Beach Boys. Many other popular musical artists are from California, including Katy Perry, Snoop Dogg, Dr. Dre, Billie Eilish, and "Weird Al" Yankovic.

So if you spend a week in Hollywood, you'll likely spot a famous person. At the very least, you can see your favorite celebrities' stars on the famous Hollywood Walk of Fame.

California also has a thriving arts scene. The state is home to several major art museums,

including Los Angeles's Getty Museum, Los Angeles County Museum of Art (LACMA), and Museum of Contemporary Art, as well as the San Francisco Museum of Modern Art.

Sports are huge in California. Californians participate in every sport you can think of,

from snow skiing to water skiing, surfing to skateboarding, and everything in between. California has over twenty major professional sports teams, more than any other state, and the oldest college football bowl game, the Rose Bowl, takes place in California.

California is also the only US state that has hosted both the Summer and Winter Olympics. The Summer Olympics took place in Los Angeles in both 1932 and 1984, while the Winter Olympics were held at Palisades Tahoe, California, in 1960. Los Angeles was also selected as the future site of the 2028 Summer Olympics.

Does all this make you want to visit California? If you go, you'll be visiting the birthplace of football star Tom Brady, astronauts Sally Ride and Ellen Ochoa, golfer Tiger Woods, and many others.

California at a Glance

Statehood: 1850

Nickname: The Golden State

Abbreviation: CA

State Motto: *Eureka* (the Greek word for "I have found it")

State Tree: California redwood

State Animal: California grizzly bear

Capital: Sacramento

Size: 163,695 square miles

Population: Over 39 million

Famous People from California: John Steinbeck (author), Serena and Venus Williams (tennis players), Olivia Rodrigo (singer and actress), Tom Hanks (actor)

Sacramento
★

State flag

State bird
California Valley quail

State flower
California poppy

FUN FACT:

Moaning Caverns, in Vallecito, California, is known for its impressive limestone formations and a haunting echo that gives the cave its name. The cavern features a massive underground chamber—it's so big, the Statue of Liberty could fit inside it!

Timeline of California

1542	Juan Rodríguez Cabrillo arrives and claims it for Spain
1769	Father Junípero Serra founds the first mission
1821	Mexico wins independence from Spain in the Mexican Revolution
1834	Mexico begins shutting down the missions
1841	The first organized overland party of US settlers arrive
1848	The United States wins the Mexican-American War and takes control of California
1850	California becomes the thirty-first US state
1854	Sacramento becomes the permanent state capital of California
1906	A huge earthquake strikes near San Francisco, killing about three thousand people
1910	Hollywood becomes part of the city of Los Angeles
1937	The Golden Gate Bridge is completed
1955	Disneyland opens in Anaheim, California
1962	Cesar Chavez forms the United Farm Workers Association
1976	Steve Jobs and Steve Wozniak start Apple Computers in Los Altos
2024	Death Valley experiences its hottest month ever recorded in July, with an average twenty-four-hour temperature of 108.5 degrees Fahrenheit

Timeline of the World

1558 — Elizabeth I becomes queen of England

1770 — Ludwig van Beethoven is born in Bonn, Germany

1793 — Eli Whitney invents the cotton gin

1821 — Panama, Guatemala, and Santo Domingo gain independence from Spain

1833 — Slavery is abolished in the British Empire

1851 — A gold rush begins in Australia

1865 — Slavery is abolished in the United States

1869 — The Transcontinental Railroad is completed

1903 — The first modern Major League Baseball World Series takes place—the Boston Red Sox beat the Pittsburgh Pirates

1914 — World War I begins

1939 — World War II begins

1969 — Neil Armstrong becomes the first person to walk on the moon

1976 — The Tangshan Earthquake strikes China, killing at least 242,000 people

1983 — Sally Ride becomes the first American woman in space

2024 — A massive earthquake strikes Japan's western coast on January 1, killing at least 168 people

Bibliography

*Books for young readers

*Alexander, Heather. *Only in California: Weird and Wonderful Facts About the Golden State*. London, UK: Wide Eyed Editions, 2022.

*Anastasio, Dina. *Where Is Hollywood?* New York: Penguin Workshop, 2019.

*Holub, Joan. *What Was the Gold Rush?* New York: Penguin Workshop, 2013.

*Hoobler, Dorothy. *What Was the San Francisco Earthquake?* New York: Penguin Workshop, 2016.

*Orr, Tamra B. *California*. America the Beautiful. Third Series. New York: Scholastic Inc., 2014.

Websites

California Agricultural Production Statistics: www.cdfa.ca.gov/Statistics/

California Capitol Museum: capitolmuseum.ca.gov/

National Park Service Weather: www.nps.gov/deva/learn/nature/weather-and-climate.htm

United States Census Bureau: www.census.gov/quickfacts/californiacitycitycalifornia

USDA Climate Hubs: www.climatehubs.usda.gov/hubs/california/topic/specialty-crops-california